SÃO PAULO

BRAZIL

Jabuti Award 1994

revised edition

CALLIS
EDITORA

Text by Sergio Sister and Claudio Cerri

Translation to English by Wordware Agência de Traduções

Photos by Ary Diesendruck

78 and 79 page's photos by A. Tokitaka/Angular

Films and Printed by Morgan Internacional Ltda., Santiago, Chile

1st edition – 1993 (5,000 copies)

2nd edition – 1995 (10,000 copies)

Dados Internacionais de Catalogação na Publicação (CIP)
(Câmara Brasileira do Livro, SP, Brasil)

São Paulo - Brazil. — São Paulo : Callis, 1993.

1. São Paulo (SP) - Descrição

93-1828   CDD-918.1611

Índices para catálogo sistemático
1. São Paulo : Cidade : Descrição   918.1611

Sponsoring
BIRMANN

Callis
EDITORA

Rua Afonso Brás, 203 • 04511-010 • São Paulo • SP • Brasil
Tel.: (011) 822-2066 • Fax: (011) 829-5882

TABLE OF CONTENTS

Paulista Avenue, june 1993, from the Fundação Casper Líbero. Photo by Ary Diesendruck.

SÃO PAULO: EVERYTHING NEW

São Paulo is the gateway to modern Brazil. A city full of surprises, never hampered by change — frantic, hectic, fast, utterly committed to newness. Founded in 1554, São Paulo is propelled by the force of over 10 million dwellers, living in a huge 1.5 thousand square kilometer area. These figures rise to more than 16 million in the metropolitan area that encompasses several suburbs[1]. The population annual growth is 206 thousand in the city, and 345 thousand in the metropolitan area[2].

Over the past four centuries, São Paulo has become the most important industrial, financial and cultural center in Latin America. It is one of the fifth world's largest cities, along with Tokyo, Mexico City, New York and Shanghai.

The city is responsible for more than 15% (the metropolitan area for almost 31%) of the industrial GNP of the country, the world's ninth highest. It has a busy and advanced financial marketplace,among the first 6th in the world in some sectors such as the Futures and Trade Exchange. In addition, it fosters a very vivid cultural life, especially vigorous in music, theater and the fine arts.

São Paulo has the largest and the best of everything. Capital of the state of São Paulo, the city is the most important unit of the federation. Its US$80 billion annual GNP and per capita income of above US$8 thousand are both much higher than that of neighboring Argentina, Chile or Mexico, higher even than those of some Asian Tigers as Korea, reaching levels of countries in Europe. That is an impressive market!

However, the city is eager for more. Ready for the coming new cycle of economic growth in Brazil, São Paulo dictates where it wants to go and what its contribution will be.

Similar to first world metropolis, the city is not only the industrial heart of the country but is also becoming its economy's brain, with an escalating expressiveness in services, commerce and finances. These industries already engage more than two million people, about 60% of the total work force in the city. To make that even more evident, it is important to point out that the service industry occupies 79 million square meters of built area, while manufacturing facilities take up 28 million square meters. This is the consolidation of São Paulo's leading role in the country's economy. São Paulo is also heading towards advanced technology and highly qualified labor, focusing on ground-breaking industries.

The profile of this progress catalyzing pole has changed over the years.

São Paulo no longer grows around a single irradiating center, many nuclei have sprung, reflecting the new trends of the complex city. Despite swift urban occupation, 25% of São Paulo's territory are still unoccupied, which means there is leeway for development.

The city currently undergoes one of the greatest verticalization processes in the planet, corresponding to 120 million square meters of new area to be built. However, that is still lesser than New York and Chicago, paradigm cities for the Paulistanos (those born in São Paulo). This means plenty of opportunities in civil construction and related sectors.

São Paulo already has one of the largest urban

Viaduto Santa Ifigênia (Santa Ifigênia Viaduct)

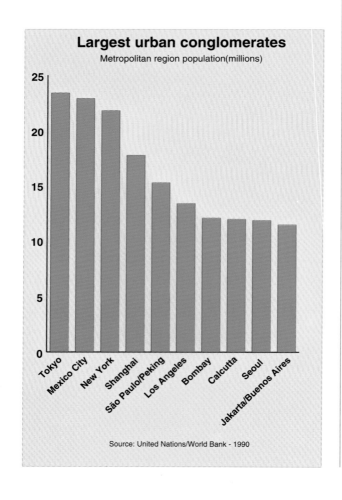

Largest urban conglomerates

Metropolitan region population(millions)

Tokyo, Mexico City, New York, Shanghai, São Paulo/Peking, Los Angeles, Bombay, Calcutta, Seoul, Jakarta/Buenos Aires

Source: United Nations/World Bank - 1990

infra-structures in Latin America, but its incessant and fast growth places a high demand on infra-structure and equipment.

Moreover, São Paulo has the bias, the talent and the culture to lead Brazil into this new stage. First, it has been the usher of the liberalization of Brazil's economy. Furthermore, being the harbor to so many migratory fluxes, its population is rare in its ethnic and cultural diversity, paralleled only by cities like New York. This favors a mentality open to change and innovation. São Paulo breaks into the future fast and decidedly.

1. The metropolitan area of São Paulo encompasses the following towns, besides São Paulo city itself: Arujá, Barueri, Biritiba-Mirim, Carapicuiba, Cajamar, Caieiras, Cotia, Diadema, Embu, Embu-Guaçu, Ferraz de Vasconcelos, Francisco Morato, Franco da Rocha, Guararema, Guarulhos, Itapecirica da Serra, Itapevi, Itaquaquecetuba, Jandira, Juquitiba, Mairiporã, Mauá, Mogi das Cruzes, Osasco, Pirapora do Bom Jesus, Poá, Ribeirão Pires, Rio Grande da Serra, Santa Isabel, Santana do Parnaíba, Santo André, São Bernardo do Campo, São Caetano do Sul, Salesópolis, Suzano, Taboão da Serra and Vargem Grande Paulista.

2. Data on population and economics were extracted from the IBGE Brazilian Institute of Geography and Statistics' Demographic Census (1990/91) and from surveys and annals of the Fundação Sistema Estadual da Análise de Dados — SEADE (State System of Data Analyses Foundation) published in *São Paulo no limiar do século XXI* (São Paulo in the threshold of the 21th century) [1992/1994].

Praça dos Arcos (Arcos' Square)

São Paulo by night

Jorge Wilheim

"São Paulo is an immense stage of opportunities for the most different interests, thanks to its size and cultural level. For instance, restaurants are excellent, there are always good shows playing and the financial market is quite active. The city, however, is not important only to those who live here. It is of fundamental importance to the whole nation, to the Mercosul (Common Market of the South Cone) and for the international business community."

Jorge Wilheim is an urban planer and is president of Emplasa, the state company responsible for the planning of the metropolitan area. Born in Trieste, Italy, he emigrated to São Paulo with his family when he was twelve. From 1975 to 1979 he coordinated the state's housing policy. From 1982 to 1984, he worked in the devising of São Paulo's Urban Plan. He was head of the State Department of Environment from 1987 to 1990.

Deutsche Bank

SÃO PAULO

Palácio dos Bandeirantes (Bandeirantes' Palace)

Preceding pages: Parque Ibirapuera (Ibirapuera Park)
Left: Rodovia dos Bandeirantes (Bandeirantes' Highway)

IDENTITY AND INTEGRATION

 Its people is the most obvious reason for São Paulo's magnitude. A cultural and ethnic diversity seldom seen elsewhere has ensured São Paulo its leading position in Latin America.

In 1934, when the city first broke the barrier of one million inhabitants, it was already a rich dough of Portuguese, Italian, African, Spanish, Arab, Jewish, German, Japanese, Armenian and many other immigrants and immigrant descendants. This promptness to welcome, absorb and assimilate the newcomers has always been present.

Nowadays, with over 10 million inhabitants, it is proud of its cosmopolitan flair, its permanent internationalization that pushes it towards the new, the modern, and sets its roots deep into the world's flux of ideas, capitals and trends.

Within its boundaries, the city houses the largest 'German industrial town' out of the Rhur and an Italian population second only to Rome when one computes the immigrants and their descendants. As a matter of fact, over twenty different ethnic groups integrate this exciting international mosaic. They have left traces in the country's history, architecture and in the generosity and diversity of its more than 2 thousand restaurants' menus. On the same table one can have side by side the feijoada, the most traditional dish of the Afro - Brazilian tradition, and the Jewish gefilte fish, the Italian macaroni and the Japanese sashimi, the Arabic kafta, Scandinavian smorgasbord and Portuguese codfish, to mention but a few options in this endless menu.

The presence of the Portuguese and Italians is overwhelming in the streets of the metropolis. However, nearly 500 thousand Japanese and Japanese descendants, 70 thousand Jews, 50 thousand Koreans, and countless Lebanese, Syrians, Spaniards, Germans, American, Scandinavians and so on, do not feel out of place. Together they create a cosmopolitan whole, rivaled only by New York.

The district of Liberdade (Freedom), with its twenty blocks of colorful architecture, dotted with restaurants, typical lanterns, the selling of kimonos and ceramics, numerous Buddhist temples, is a fine representation of the quintessence of this open city. This is the redoubt of the Japanese whose sons already account for 13% of the students enrolled in courses at the University of São Paulo, the most important in the country. Identity and integration — this is the ethnic synthesis of this manifold metropolis, that the Japanese trajectory illustrates and summarizes. This cosmopolitan trait is also visible in Bom Retiro, the Jewish neighborhood in São Paulo, and one of the most important addresses of the garment industry. In the 70's the development of a Korean settlement started, and today the Koreans already own almost two thousand garment factories. This is an example of the city's dynamism. However, nothing ever disrupts the orthodox Jews' routine. On Fridays they close their stores earlier than the Koreans and march to the synagogues. It is the Shabat.

At that very moment, not very far, a little Baghdad of three thousand stores witnesses the closing of

District of Liberdade

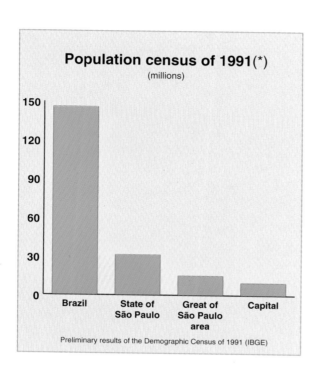

Population census of 1991(*)
(millions)

Brazil | State of São Paulo | Great of São Paulo area | Capital

Preliminary results of the Demographic Census of 1991 (IBGE)

the last deals of the day in a real Arab souk concentrated in less than 4 kilometers of streets. That is the 25 de Março street, the Phoenician heart of the town. Its cheerful commerce of houses packed with articles that pile up in anarchy preserves the tradition of competitive prices of which the Syrians and the Lebanese — charming characters of this Persian market inlaid in the city — are so proud.

As hectic as the Arab neighborhood is the district of Bixiga. Bixiga, Brás and Barra Funda are the Italian tripod of São Paulo. Music, wine, good food are synonymous to the Italian restaurants in Bixiga. On week-ends, they prove the neighborhood deserves to be called "Piccola Italia". That is the place to go for pizza, wine and pasta. São Paulo eats, every month, 7.6 million pizzas!

Templo Budista Hompa Homgw Anji do Brasil (Buddhist Temple)

Spanish festival

Pizzeria 1900

**Preceding pages: Catedral Metropolitana de São Paulo
(São Paulo's Metropolitan Cathedral)
Right: Sinagoga da Congregação Beneficente Sefardita Paulista
(Synagogue of the Sephardim Beneficent Congregation of São Paulo)**

PERMANENT RECONSTRUCTION

 From above, the fifth largest city in the world is astonishing. In spite of being this gigantic human mix, paved on cement and asphalt, there is still plenty of empty space in São Paulo. According to official data, 20% of the total 1.5 thousand square kilometers of the city remain unoccupied.

Concerned with a more rational occupation for the future, the city is now engaged in the discussion of a new urban plan. One of the proposals is to have it divided into 15 macro-areas, each with its own real estate plan, accommodating building density and infra-structure.

According to present legislation, 70% of the total city area cannot be occupied with buildings more than twice the area of the plot. That is why São Paulo, in spite of its powerful architecture is not an extremely vertical city. Only in 10% of the city area there can be buildings four times the total area of the plot, whereas in Chicago or New York this rate is as high as 20%.

Experts believe that a policy to privilege verticalization associated with additional fees for constructed areas superior to the area of the plot, will significantly increase the availability of real estate. That means a reduction of the housing deficit in the city — estimated in 600 thousand to 1 million housing units. This could be an important lever to the marketplace, since more than 200 million square meters would be made available for building.

São Paulo thus has a very good outlook for the year 2,020, with an average of 8 million square meters built annually, mantaining the average of the first half of the 1990's decade.

This is the perspective for a city that never stops, that changes and renews itself day to day, never losing however its ties with the past. It is the best expression of the Paulistanos' entrepreneurship. The city is well aware that being modern does not necessarily mean turning its back to tradition.

After all, today's scenery is the outcome of the adventure our ancestors engaged in on the top of the hill where the city started in 1554 and which overlooks the Anhangabaú Valley.

This valley is the historic heart of the city, and for decades was the center of the economic and cultural activities of the metropolis. It is delimited by the Municipal Theatre, the city's majestic theater, and the Chá Viaduct, built in 1892, named after the hill planted with 40 thousand tea plants where it started. This ancient nucleus gradually lost its significance. Industrialization boosted the multiplication of the city arteries. Little by little the Anhangabaú Valley was suffocated by the frantic traffic of over 15 thousand vehicles per hour.

In December 1991, the old center recovered its post-card face. After a five year remodeling, the 77 thousand square meters (11 thousand of green) were reopened to the 1,5 million people who daily cross the center of the city. Cars and buses, that had pushed the young and the old away, now run underground, in 570 meter tunnels that connect the northern and the southern sections of the city.

Casa das Rosas - Galeria Estatual de Arte (State Art Gallery)

The revival of São Paulo's historic center is now irreversible with the inauguration of the new Anhangabaú Valley. The city administration has plans to liberate more than 800 thousand square meters around the valley for more sophisticated buildings. It is important to point out that São Paulo is always in a process of reconstruction and recycling, changing whenever needed. This is the reason for its eclectic architecture that astonishes the visitor at every turn.

A few minutes away from the historic center are the most elegant residential areas, comparable to American and European suburbs. In this area, known as the Jardins[1], there are 50 square meters of greenery per capita; houses average 60.5 square meters per dweller, and the standard of living is that of the upper middle class in most developed countries.

One may say the Jardins is the residential counterpart of Avenida Paulista, the most important financial artery in the city. It is only 2.6 kilometers long, but it is the address of many of the largest banks in the country, two businesses' federations and hundreds of corporations. Real estate along the avenue alone is worth $7 billion, not to mention the patrimony of the Museu de Arte de São Paulo. MASP's art collection is worth over one billion dollars and it is praised for its impressionist master pieces.

The fortune addresses in cities as large as São Paulo are often related to the big traffic axles. It used to be so with the Anhangabaú Valley, later with Avenida Paulista and nowadays with the road alongside the Pinheiros River. It is there that corporate capital and brains are heading — a privileged rectangular area served by four of the most important avenues in the city: Jucelino Kubistchek, Morumbi, Luís Carlos Berrini and Nações Unidas.

It is not only easy access that magnetizes business to the Southwestern section of the city. Modern concepts of integrated management require large areas — often over 1,000 square meters per floor, impossible to find in other already crowded commercial areas of the city.

From 1986 to 1991, nearly one hundred large corporations moved their head offices to modern buildings near the Marginal Pinheiros; companies such as the Dutch Philips, the American Dow Chemical, Coca-Cola, and Johnson & Johnson, and the German Hoescht, as well as Japanese companies such as Fuji Photo and the Swiss Nestlé. Finance conglomerates like the Deutsche Bank and the Chase Manhattan also have their offices there. Since 1990, the area has concentrated almost 70 per cent of the new office buildings in the city. This is a trend that is likely to continue in the 90's; and this area that used to be a low building density area will rapidly be occupied.

1. One of the most elegant areas of the city, Os Jardins (the gardens) are the generic denomination of the neighborhoods Jardim América, Jardim Paulistano, Jardim Europa e Cerqueira César, a rectangle sided by the avenues: Rebouças, Paulista, Nove de Julho and Brigadeiro Faria Lima.

Palácio das Indústrias — (City Hall)

District of Alto de Pinheiros

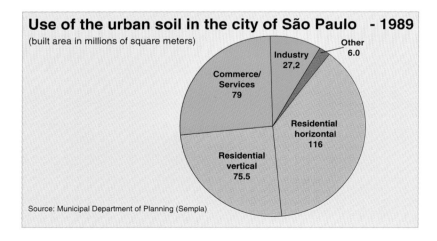

Use of the urban soil in the city of São Paulo - 1989
(built area in millions of square meters)

Industry
27,2

Other
6.0

Commerce/
Services
79

Residential
horizontal
116

Residential
vertical
75.5

Source: Municipal Department of Planning (Sempla)

Engenheiro Luís Carlos Berrini Avenue

TUNED AND CONNECTED

From the political effervescence of the coffee economy in the 20's to the urban dynamism of industrialization in the 30's and 40's, São Paulo has always set the pace for Brazil's economic clockwork. Today, the city generates a gross national product of $80 billion, and sets a new paradigm of leadership: the laborious locomotive metaphor is replaced by the intelligent brain that plans, decides and commands, via fax and computers.

Like other metropolis such as London, New York, Chicago or Milan, São Paulo emerges as the advanced managerial pole of Brazil's capitalism. The hegemony of services (trade and financial) is irreversible, but it does not exclude other industries. While it has become the strategic center of management and services, that unites the domestic market and connects it to the world, the city is, nevertheless, proud of its status as the most complex industrial compound in Latin America.

Staging most of the country's trade and decision-making, the city catalyzes and multiplies business options. Its bias to commerce and services is reflected in the expansion of shopping malls, wholesale and outlet centers, as and in the multiplication of franchises and partnerships. It is obvious why two thirds of the current job offer in the city is in the service industry and why 65% of the international firms in the country have their management in the metropolitan area.

The city's sophisticated commerce is comparable to New York's, Rome's and Tokyo's. The glittering stores in the Jardins could be taken for those on Via dei Condotti, Rome, with their exhibits of Giorgio Armani, Benetton, Dior, Charles Jourdan and Pierre Balmain. This is a sign of the internationalization process and the struggle for competitiveness Brazil's economy undergoes at the moment.

São Paulo has a network of 55 thousand stores, 13 shopping malls and over 60 thousand service companies. A per capita income of $8,164 per year, close to that of some European countries, and 50% larger than South Korea's, makes the city an attractive market to new commercial projects. Indicators of family income compatible with those of modern economies help evaluate its potential demand for goods and services. Over 90% of the 2 million households in the city have TV sets, 89% have refrigerators, 44% have saving accounts and 35% have cars.

This potential is partly what is going to mold the real estate scenery in the future. Over the last years there has been a remarkable multiplication of commercial nuclei and wholesale outlets. This plays a leading role in redefining and expanding regional trends. About an average of 140 large businesses in the service industry are licensed, every year, in São Paulo, since 1989. This total represents over 2 million square meters of new

Preceding pages: Centro Velho (Downtown)
Marginal do Rio Pinheiros (Road along the Pinheiros River)
Campus of São Paulo University
Left: Eldorado Shopping Center

SÃO PAULO

Store of the Vila Romana clothes manufacturer

buildings— at least 25% of which destined exclusively to commerce. Together investments in real estate and commerce redefine the city's profile. The city is on its way to having many and diversified nuclei, a dense industrial basis and a keen commercial bias. São Paulo is an urban center tuned to international standards of production and expenditure, as only fitting to a truly cosmopolitan city.

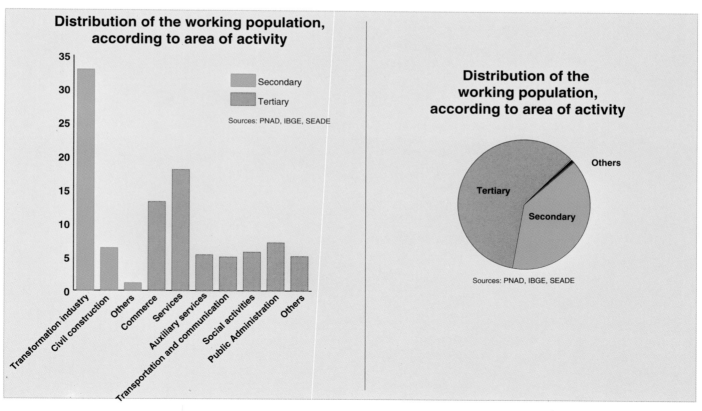

Distribution of the working population, according to area of activity

Secondary
Tertiary

Sources: PNAD, IBGE, SEADE

Transformation industry
Civil construction
Others
Commerce
Services
Auxiliary services
Transportation and communication
Social activities
Public Administration
Others

Distribution of the working population, according to area of activity

Others
Tertiary
Secondary

Sources: PNAD, IBGE, SEADE

Parque Ecológico do Tietê (Tietê Ecological Park)

THE METROPOLIS AND NATURE

Committed to modernization and therefore subjected to its byproducts, São Paulo has developed technologies to deal with the hazardous effects of urban expansion (especially pollution). With 7% of Brazil's total population, the city disposes of 1.1 thousand tons of organic waste daily in the Tietê River[1], the river that served as route to the settlers heading inland in the beginning of the 17th century.

A daring project — the most important project of recuperation of hydrous resources in Latin America — intends, by 1998, to reduce this polluting load by 50%. Subsequent depuration, biological and landscape recovery efforts will be carried out for three years after the first stage is completed. Life might be restored in the river.

The project's budget is $900 million, half of which to be provided by the state. The Inter-American Development Bank, IBD, will finance the remaining 50%. This amount will pay for five processing plants, two thousand kilometers of sewage system and 553 kilometers of main sewage collecting canals, a paramount program private enterprise will implement.

Additional $500 million — half of which provided by the BNDS (National Bank of Social Development) — will be used in controlling the industrial waste, responsible for 30% of the polluting material currently dumped in the river. Cetesb (State Company of Technology and Sanitation), has already surveyed the 1,250 companies responsible for 80% of the industrial waste in the Tietê. Equipped to perform advanced monitoring of pollutants, Cetesb's policy is to see to the implementation of processing devices. That creates a demand for environmental technology.

Air pollution also requires keen and highly sophisticated monitoring. Daily, 5.5 million kilos of carbon monoxide are cast over the 100 square kilometer downtown area. There are 4.5 million vehicles in the metropolitan area (30% of the nation's total fleet). The city's main arteries show warning boards informing the population of the air quality around the clock. This ensures the prompt collaboration of the population whenever rerouting traffic is necessary. New York city has later imported and adopted this technology.

São Paulo is also getting ready to innovate in one of the most crucial challenges mega-cities have to face: garbage collecting and processing. São Paulo annually produces 4.3 million tons of waste of which at least 30% are recyclable Twenty-three neighborhoods have already adopted a system of selective collection that allows the recycling of organic waste for compost.

As important as controlling and recycling pollutants it is preserving the city's natural resources. That is why city governments have tried to discipline urban occupation of the South Zone where most water sources are located. The area they are concerned with covers 532 square kilometer, larger than some small countries such as Andorra, Granada and Barbados. It is there that the rivers, brooks and springs that feed the city's major reservoirs — Billings and Guarapiranga, a 65 square kilometer water surface — start. The

Air quality information board

Cantareira water treatment plant

Recicling System

sources in the South Zone together with the 5.6 hectares of remains of the Atlantic forest in the Cantareira mountain range is the main link between the metropolis and nature.

1. Three rivers run through the city of São Paulo: Tietê, Pinheiros and Tamanduateí.

São Paulo's green belt
Preceding pages: Guarapiranga Reservoir

THE RURAL SIDE

 Recent figures for São Paulo State's agriculture do not surprise those familiar with the fact that São Paulo is not only highly industrialized but also a major food producer. In 1993, for instance, the state produced 159,2 million tons of sugar cane, 52% of the country's total, more than great producers like Cuba and China. About 12.5 million of the 14.5 million tons of oranges produced in Brazil came from São Paulo. In addition, the state was responsible for 18% of the coffee, 10.5% of the corn and 4.8% of the soya Brazil produced. It has 8% of the country's livestock and grows most everything: beans, rice, cotton, and peanuts. Really astonishing are the figures on agriculture in the city of São Paulo. There is a São Paulo that is quite different from the hectic capital of busy traffic and people in a hurry everyone is familiar with. Inlaid in this cement giant there is a rural belt that covers 549 square kilometers, a little over a third of the whole municipality. In this other São Paulo there are about 50 thousand people whose pace and life style are a counterpoint to the urban population's hasty routine.

Despite being a minority in area and population, the green belt is responsible for 15% of the vegetables grown in the state. 487 tons of potatoes and 350 thousand of tons of fruit - especially high quality peaches—are grown there per year.

Those who think São Paulo is synonymous to steel and pollution may be startled to know that it is the biggest flower producer in Brazil. Its chrysanthemums and orchids are sold all over the country, and part is exported abroad.

The green belt, however, is not the only connection between the cement São Paulo and the rural world. Decisions that directly affect production are made here, in the 1,700 offices of big agro-industrial companies that run their business with one eye on the land and another on the urban marketplace. At least 45 thousand businessmen of the state's modern agriculture live in the city.

Still, it is as a major agricultural entrepôt that the city shares its dynamism with the country. The Companhia de Entrepostos e Armazéns Gerais (Company of Entrepôts and Warehouses) of São Paulo, Ceagesp, is a 655 thousand square meter food distribution compound, the largest in Latin America. With warehouses and pavilions that total an area of 220 thousand square meters, Ceagesp has a storage capacity of over 1.2 million tons, nearly 12% of the total storage capacity of the state. Daily, over 10 thousand tons of food are traded in this gigantic entrepôt, amid the noise of a buying and selling dynamics that involves more than 50 thousand people. People and products from all over the country make this spectacle the synthesis of São Paulo's spirit.

Flower stand along Dr. Arnaldo Avenue

Mercado Municipal (Municipal Market)

READY FOR THE MODERN

Even though there has been a concentrated effort towards decentralization in the country, São Paulo is still the major manufacturing pole in Brazil. Alone, it is responsible for no less than 15.4% of the industrial GNP. This rises to more than 30% if we consider the whole metropolitan area. The state of São Paulo is responsible for half the country's industrial production.

The city manufactures from the most basic products such as processed food, garments, shoes and beverages to car parts and capital goods to the most sophisticated electronic equipment. São Paulo shelters part of the facilities of giants such as Volkswagen, IBM, Gessy Lever, Metal Leve, Vilares, Alpargatas either in traditional neighborhoods as Ipiranga and Lapa or in the new conquered frontiers in the South Zone. Figures are higher if we consider the metropolitan area, Osasco, Barueri and the so-called ABCD that includes the cities of Santo André, São Bernardo do Campo, São Caetano and Diadema.

Of the working population, 25.2% are employed in the transformation industry and 2.9% in the major construction works.

This means industry still plays a major part in São Paulo's economy.

In the past, industry had an even more significant role. Like the Monument to the Bandeirantes, in the Ibirapuera, the Pacaembu Stadium, the Anhangabaú Valley and the skyscrapers in the old center, factory chimneys used to be the emblem of the city. A landmark that made visitors sure of their whereabouts.

In 1970, the metropolitan area reached the mark of 43.5% of the industrial GNP. But, as with Chicago, Boston and other highly industrialized cities around the planet, the moment came when São Paulo had to give in to other areas. Consequently there was a remarkable expansion to the interior of the state, especially along the Paraíba Valley, Campinas and to other states, as Minas Gerais. Little was lost, nevertheless. The coming of the high technology industries has counterbalanced the moving out of traditional industries. Furthermore, most leading industries, with the exception of the electric and electronic segments that benefit from the Free Zone tax incentives in Manaus, are all located in the area. This is where Brazil creates the most in terms of advanced technologies and managerial procedures and that is why experts believe the city will keep its leading position in the industrial sector. São Paulo will remain a factory town.

CET - Cia de Engenharia de Tráfego (Traffic Department)

Subway's Control Panel

Kibon — (Food Industry)

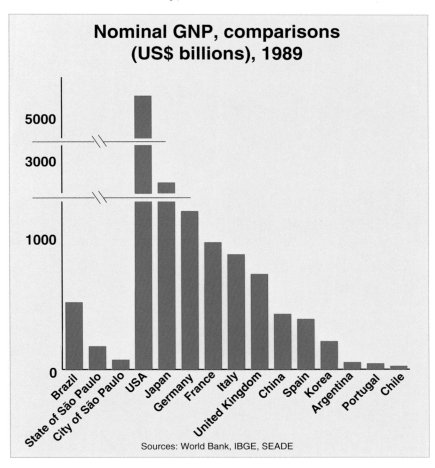

Nominal GNP, comparisons (US$ billions), 1989

Sources: World Bank, IBGE, SEADE

SERVICES

Numerical data on São Paulo are impressive: it has 6.4 thousand kilometers of paved roads, and every third minute another meter is paved. At least 4.5 million cars drive through its arteries. The 10 thousand buses make 40 million trips a year, transporting almost 2 billion passengers. São Paulo's subway has the Guinness record of more passengers per square kilometer. A child is born every second and a half. A plane lands on one of its three airports every three minutes, while in its 1,500 thousand bank agencies 55 checks are cleared every second. The city makes over 36 million phone calls a day.

There is consensus among politicians, government, population and businessmen that such numbers, however, are not yet what everybody would like them to be. The expansion of the metropolitan area demands investments in three major strategic sectors: telecommunication, transportation and social structure.

There has been an amazing development in telephony over the last decades. The 3.7 million telephone lines in 1989 meant 217.3 terminals for every 1,000 inhabitants, while in 1980 that number was 183.3, well above the national average of 60 terminals per 1,000 inhabitants.

In Barueri, one of the cities in the metropolitan area, there was a leap of 243% in the period, that is, from 69.5 for each 1,000 inhabitants in 1980 to 237.1 terminals per thousand in 1989.

Yet, the region's growth has been — as in most of the country — faster than the increase in the number of telephone lines available. In other words, demand grows faster than offer. Starting in 1986, new expansion plans were implemented, but the necessary increment in the network was neglected. Hence, in 1995, at least 100 thousand terminals sold have not been installed yet. There is a repressed demand above 1.5 million terminals. Resources will be obtained with a policy of international financing, partnership with the private sector or partial or total privatization of the telephone companies.

At the same time cellular telephony will continue to grow, the exploitation of which may in the future be in the hands of private enterprises. Estimates are for a market of 500 thousand subscriptions, with a revenue of above $2 billion annually.

As to transportation, investments will convert to the bus fleet and the subway. São Paulo wants to provide a better and faster transportation to the 3.4 million passengers that use public transportation daily.

In 1991, 71.3% of the users depended on the ten thousand urban buses (57.6 percent on urban lines, and 17.6 percent on inter municipal lines). A little less then 24% of the passengers used the subway and 5% the suburban trains.

Regardless of who is next in the city administration, the trend is to expand the services. The need to improve the rate of 1 bus for each 1,000 inhabitants will also mean an increase in demand for buses from the automotive industry and consequently more jobs.

Most bets, however, are placed on the expansion of the subway network. Today, there are two major

Estação da Luz (train station)

lines connecting the North to the South, and the East to the West of the city, and a short branch under Avenida Paulista that will connect Vila Prudente to the bohemian neighborhood of Vila Madalena.

The blueprints for two other major lines are been prepared: one will connect the town center to the populous neighborhood of Pinheiros, in the West, with a connection to the railway that runs parallel to the Pinheiros River, where new stations will be build; and a branch of the basic North-South line will go to the industrial ABCD, starting at the industrial pole in Diadema.

The government plans to implement a suburban railway compound, to the advantage of the whole South Zone. A large terminal on Florida Street, will receive subway and railway trains, and a new 33 kilometers long line of trolley buses,

São Paulo is also getting ready for a leap in what has been called 'the social debt'.

In 1993, the state had 753 hospitals and a little less then 100 thousand hospital beds, a rate of 3 beds per 1,000 inhabitants, below to Argentina's, Israel's, and Portugal's rate, much better than Chile's, Mexico's and Korea's rate, but very modest when compared to Japan's, Germany or Sweden's.

In education, illiteracy reached 11% and the number of classrooms — 90 thousand — was absolutely insufficient.

In spite of the great improvement in statistics that has taken place lately, the city, the state and the country will tend to concentrate efforts till the mid-nineties on recovering the public sector's investing capacity, to improve health, sanitation, education and housing standards.

Manabu Mabe

'São Paulo gives me a feeling of freedom I don't experience in any other capital in the world; not even in Rome, Paris, New York or Tokyo. Here cosmopolitanism is absolute, and there is room for everyone. This space for identity is key to creation. The city is also full of motion: intense motion, driven by diversity, the signature of the end of this century. I come from the country. This motion has imprinted its mark on my painting. I need it to produce.'

Manabu Mabe is one of the Brazilian painters of strongest presence in the international marketplace. His canvases of intense motion and color are found in the most important museums in the world. Mabe is a veteran in the international circuit of the arts He was first prize in the 1957 Paris Biennial. He was born in Kumamoto, south of Japan, and arrived in Brazil in the mid 30's. His family went to the country to work in coffee farms. As a boy he helped his parents in the fields, but was always drawing. In October 1957, Manabu came to São Paulo. Two years later he would win he city's Biennial, and ten days later the Paris Biennial.

Estação Sé — Metrô (Subway - Sé Station)

Estação da Luz (train station)
Preceding pages: 23 de Maio Avenue
Right: Estação Júlio Prestes (Júlio Prestes train station)

THE BEST OF CULTURE

Nothing can paint a better picture of São Paulo's cultural effervescence than the newspaper's entertainment section. On a typical Saturday in a cold August, a newspaper with large circulation listed:

- 31 plays for the regular public and 12 for children, playing on 42 theater-houses. One of them was, for instance, Shakespeare's 'Midsummer Night's Dream' staged by Cacá Rosset, the same performance presented in Central Park, New York.

- Forty-eight films, for every taste, in 143 cinemas and 18 especial movie rooms

- Mozart's Don Giovanni was at the Teatro Municipal. This 80-year-old theater is the pride of the city's eclectic architecture, a fusion of neoclassic-classic and *art nouveau* that houses memorable seasons of classic music and ballet.

- 23 art exhibits, four of which very special: Joseph Beuyes, an important contemporary German artist, Italian-Brazilian Alfredo Volpi, Swiss-Brazilian Mira Schendel and Cildo Meireles who has just returned from the Kassel Documenta in Germany

- Three ballets

- 12 Brazilian pop music and 5 Jazz performances.

São Paulo, a real metropolis, offers its large and heterogeneous public a wide array of options to please not only the Paulistanos, but also the tourists that come by the thousands to visit this gigantic city.

When the main attraction is someone like Luciano Pavarotti or Zubin Mehta conducting The New York Philarmonic Orchestra, the city prepares one of the huge soccer stadiums or the fields on the city parks to receive the crowd.

Even at hard times, the three main classical music seasons — the one at the Teatro da Cultura Artística, the one at the Mozarteum and the other at the City Hall — never lose their quality or their public. The concerts at Cultura Artística take place in two concert halls, one seats 1156 and a smaller one seats 322, and date from the 20's, with performances from March to November.

On Sundays a little patience is required from those who want to visit the Museu de Arte de São Paulo, (MASP), one of the places in São Paulo that receives the most visitors. It has two auditoriums, four temporary exhibit areas and a priceless collection. It has a remarkable collection of Impressionist paintings, a highly praised suit of sculptures by Degas and some gems by Rafael, Botticelli, Goya, Velasquez, Rembrandt, Poussin, Chardin, Delacroix, Cézanne and Van Gogh.

When the museum has an especial exhibit such as a collection of Picasso's engravings, a visiting selection from the Modern Art Museum of New York (MoMA) or a Russian or Israeli treasure, people line up in front of the museum, waiting for a chance to get in.

São Paulo has the excellent Museum of Sacred Art, with precious pieces of the Brazilian Baroque; the State Collection, a Sculpture Museum and the Museum of Contemporary Art. Every other year, since 1951, it hosts the world famous International Art Biennial of São Paulo, and the beautiful

Museu Paulista — Ipiranga (Museum Paulista)

Teatro Municipal (Municipal Theater)

pavilion designed by Oscar Niemeyer is visited by thousands of people.

Private enterprise funds the Biennial, and the movie, dance and jazz festivals. This is stimulated by the tax incentive laws. The municipality (Law 10.923) that reduces real estate taxes for those who invest in cultural and educational projects. Federal legislation (Law 8.131) provides for reduction on income taxes. The cultural outlook is auspicious, especially because of the educational structure of the city and the state: Most units of the São Paulo University (USP), the country's most important high education compound, of the Catholic University, (PUC), and the Mackenzie University are located in the city. Also in the city we have the Free University of Music and five orchestras. With the other universities in the state, including the Unicamp and 16 private universities, there were 500 thousand students enrolled in 1992, approximately one third of the college students in the country.

Monumento às Bandeiras (Monument to the Pioneers)

**Pinacoteca do Estado de São Paulo
(São Paulo State Art Collection)**

MASP — Museu de Arte de São Paulo (São Paulo Art Museum)

LEISURE

It is certainly a meaningless stereotype the notion that São Paulo is a non-stop workaholic factory-town. The high rate of occupancy in its 2,770 hotels (140 of high standard) is not due only to business but also, to a large extent, to the choice entertainment the city has to offer.

Besides the plentiful cultural life of cinemas, theaters and art galleries, São Paulo has a myriad of leisure options.

Leisure starts early in the city at inviting sports facilities in the most beautiful parks like Ibirapuera, Morumbi, Aclimação and Previdência.

The Ibirapuera Park is, no doubt, one of the favorite and best equipped parks in town. It has special tracks for jogging, multi-purpose courts, play-grounds, three museums and a planetarium. Every neighborhood has at least one sports club or gym. Totaling 65 major sports clubs and 600 small clubs and gymnasiums, mostly any sport for any taste and standard.

The city watches important soccer tournaments in huge stadiums: Morumbi (150 thousand seats), Pacaembu (60 thousand) and Parque Antarctica (30 thousand), Canindé (30 thousand) or Parque São Jorge (18 thousand).

São Paulo made important contributions to the volleyball team that was champion in the 1992 Olympic games in Barcelona, to the Brazilian basketball team, and to the team that conquered the 1994 World Soccer Championship in the United States. It is strong in judo, tennis and boxing.

A kind of energy center to Brazil and Latin America, São Paulo is a show-town also for business. It hosts from industry and technology to book and furniture shows. The best places for these huge fairs are the Parque Anhembi or the Parque da Bienal. On Sundays, in neighborhoods like the Italian Bexiga, stands along the streets sell antique pieces, and MASP's lobby also stages an antiques' fair.

At night São Paulo goes dancing. There are many rock-and-roll places as the Aeroanta and the Columbia, besides more traditional night clubs for ball dancing or just cozy, soft-music places for romancing.

To meet friends and celebrate, Paulistanos prefer bars. At least 200 of them are rated as first class places, one totally different from the other, from the place for a sandwich and a beer, to a pub, to the favorite meeting places of artists and intellectuals or politicians, and single's bars. The swing of the bars in the Jardins or at the Vilaboim square, in Higienópolis is a must.

But it is at the dinner table that São Paulo is at its best. It is easy to have a good meal out. Foreigners generally love the 'churrascarias' (barbecue places) because it is hard to find elsewhere in the world meat as good as Bassi's, Wessel's or Rubaiyat's[1]. Italians can hardly believe the quality of the Italian food served at Ca'd'Oro, Fasano, Jardim de Napoli, Mássimo, and the exquisite pizzas at Cantina Speranza, Castelões or Babbo Giovanni. There are hundreds

Preceding pages: Teatro Municipal (Municipal Theater)
Left: Maksoud Plaza Hotel

Paulo Maluf

"São Paulo is the one thousand people city. With an open heart São Paulo received immigrants from all over Brazil, and all over the world. It is also a city of opportunities. People who believe in what they do and do it with dedication will be rewarded in São Paulo. It is also a city of challenges and immense transformation. It showed to Brazil the road to industrialization and today it is the strategic center of commerce, big events and technology. I love São Paulo and to it I dedicate my very best, because I have faith on the "Paulistanos", that know where they want to go and choose the right way to do it."

Mayor of São Paulo twice, governor of the state and federal deputy, Paulo Maluf is one of the typical sides of São Paulo. Son of Lebanese immigrants that succeeded through commerce and industry, he did all his studies in São Paulo.

Street Market

Performance in the Ibirapuera Park

of tratorias, and cantinas, as well as German, French, Japanese Portuguese, Spanish, Chinese, Tai, Jewish and Indian food, and, of course, the best Brazilian cuisine.

1. Two of the most reliable restaurant ratings are: *Guia de São Paulo*, published by Editora Abril, and *100 Restaurantes*, by Josimar Melo, published by the Folha de São Paulo.

Fasano restaurant

Burle Marx Park

Simba Safari (Zoo park)

Preceding pages: Cícero Pompeu de Toledo Soccer Stadium

Jardim Botânico (Botanical Garden)

Having fun in São Paulo

Massimo Ferrari

'São Paulo is one of the five most important addresses in the gastronomic world. Here you can taste every flavor, every language of the international cuisine. It is a very savory city, a temptation to taste. One thing I like is to go to the different neighborhoods seeking for its best cuisine. It is incredible how you can find here a little bit of everything from every corner of the Earth.'

Massimo Ferrari is the best known restaurateur in São Paulo. He was born in Premosello, a small village in the Italian Piedmont. The Ferraris came to Brazil after World War II. They opened the first meat place in the city: Os Pampas. Later, they started the Cabanas, still run by mama Maria Ferrari. In 1976, they opened Massimo, the symbol of good Italian cuisine in São Paulo, a favorite place for politicians, businessman and gourmets.

Having fun in São Paulo

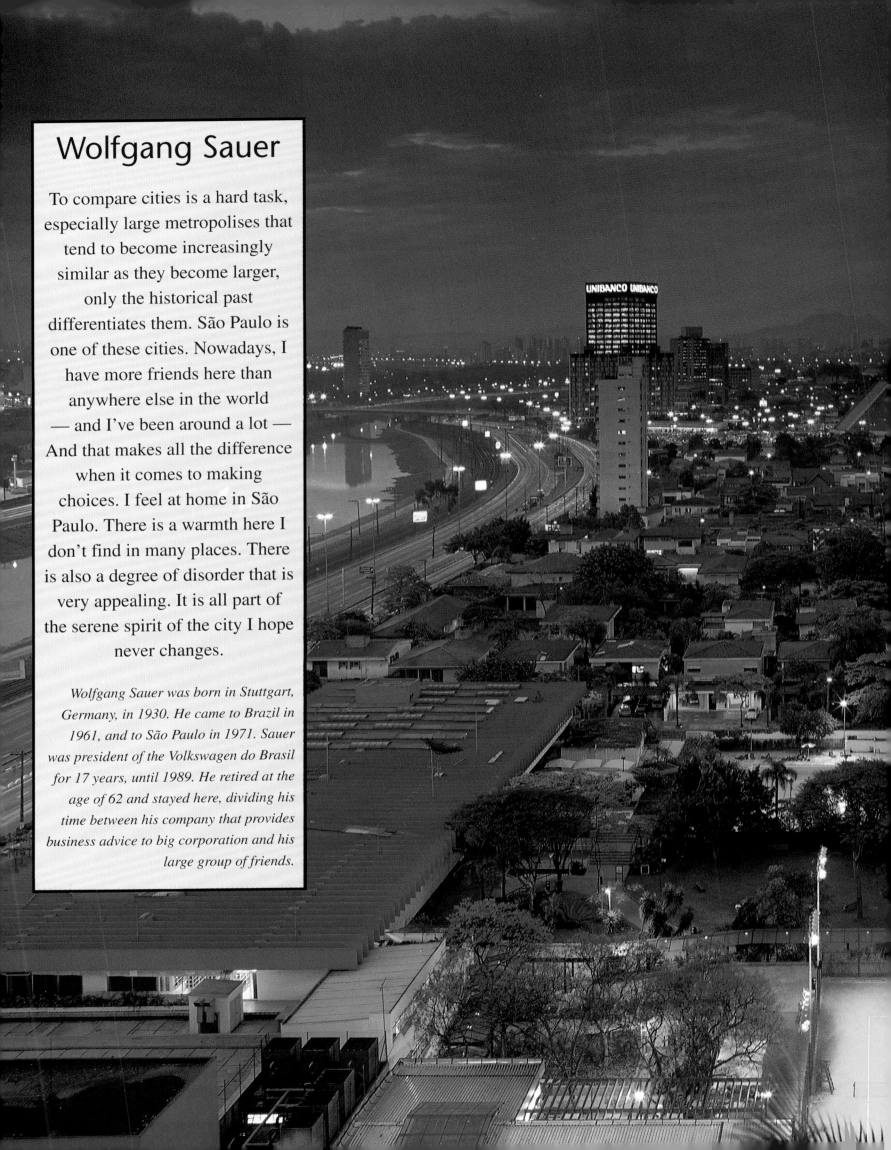

Wolfgang Sauer

To compare cities is a hard task, especially large metropolises that tend to become increasingly similar as they become larger, only the historical past differentiates them. São Paulo is one of these cities. Nowadays, I have more friends here than anywhere else in the world — and I've been around a lot — And that makes all the difference when it comes to making choices. I feel at home in São Paulo. There is a warmth here I don't find in many places. There is also a degree of disorder that is very appealing. It is all part of the serene spirit of the city I hope never changes.

Wolfgang Sauer was born in Stuttgart, Germany, in 1930. He came to Brazil in 1961, and to São Paulo in 1971. Sauer was president of the Volkswagen do Brasil for 17 years, until 1989. He retired at the age of 62 and stayed here, dividing his time between his company that provides business advice to big corporation and his large group of friends.

THE MEDIA

São Paulo is Brazil's best-informed metropolis. It is impossible to walk or drive along its streets without been hit by information. Sound, light, colors, images, outdoors, newsstands, communication is omnipresent.

26 AM radio stations and an equal number of FM radio stations wake the Paulistano to tell what is up in town, in his country, and in the world: politics, economy, sports, fashion and money, music and manias. There are weather forecast stations, stations for time and traffic information. For music, tune to stations like Jovem Pan, Eldorado and Bandeirantes. To escape the anxiety caused by the world's news, turn the dial to Radio Cultura AM for a Beethoven sonata; heat up with rock-and-roll on 89 radio or listen to a preacher and pray a little.

But news will eventually get hold of you. Who can resist the many magazines for every age, taste and interest, and the appeal of the fresh newspaper headlines in the newsstands that pop up at every corner?

Fourteen daily papers are published in the city. Some are nationwide circulation newspapers like O Estado de São Paulo, A Folha de São Paulo and A Gazeta Mercantil, with a total circulation of 1.5 million copies.

There are 62 weekly papers, 50 come out every fortnight, 25 every month and there are several specialized publications, directed to specific audiences like business people, professionals, or dwellers of a certain neighborhood. The total number of newspapers that come out daily in the metropolitan area is 22; weekly, 74; fortnightly, 48; and monthly, 21.

The two major weekly magazines in Brazil are published in São Paulo: *Veja* and *IstoÉ*, a total circulation of over one million copies, there are also a myriad of other titles like *Elle, Vogue, Playboy, Exame, Marie Claire, Claudia, Quatro Rodas,* and *Interview*. São Paulo has not one but several major art magazines like the *Revista do Museu de Arte de São Paulo, Guia das Artes,* and others.

Along the streets it is impossible to keep the eye from looking at the outdoors and neon signs, or even the graffiti on the walls along the Paulista Avenue tunnel that authorities ended up reserving for this purpose.

Television in São Paulo, as in the rest of the country, is a big deal. There are seven regular channels, five of which broadcast in the city, and UHF 935 cable channels and 11 by microwave with international broadcasting from 10 diferent countries).

It is true that the major TV network in the country centers its operation in Rio de Janeiro, but it is São Paulo that provides the two most important ends of the business: the largest audience and the largest publicity revenue.

In addition, São Paulo, along with Brasília, is a major source of journalistic data in the country, because it is here that decisions are made on business and culture.

Preceding pages: A Hebraica Club
Left: One of the radio and television towers at Paulista Avenue

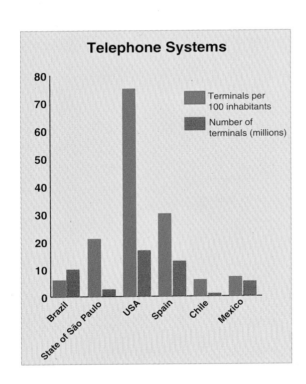

Telephone Systems

Legend:
- Terminals per 100 inhabitants
- Number of terminals (millions)

Categories: Brazil, State of São Paulo, USA, Spain, Chile, Mexico

A natural consequence is a concentration of news and publicity agencies right here. Of the 62 largest agencies in the country, 32 (52%) are located in the city. Rio de Janeiro has 10 major agencies (16%).

Newstand

Folha de São Paulo **newspaper's**

WEALTH AHEAD!

The financial heart of Brazil also beats in São Paulo, the money city.

This very sophisticated and lucrative system has to deal with some truly arduous tasks, such as: a) financing the debts incurred by the Union, the states and municipalities; b) supplying private businesses with capital; c) managing the national savings so that it increases in value or is protected from inflation through a series of options in interest rendering accounts and investment funds; d) providing alternatives for attracting foreign funds to the country through its active stock market or by issuing bonds out side the country.

The financial structure of São Paulo is of astounding proportions: 1) Of the ten largest Brazilian banks, six have their headquarters in São Paulo. These are enormous conglomerates such as Bradesco, Banespa, Itaú, Nossa Caixa Nosso Banco, Unibanco and Safra. If the 1994 deposits of all these banks were to be added, the sum would amount to over US$20 billion (1). Considering all bank branches, including those of banks which have headquarters in other cities or countries, the city holds about 1,500 bank agencies. 2) São Paulo has about 150 brokerage firms and 170 dealers. 3) The São Paulo stock market negotiates stocks of about 600 companies through 140 brokerage firms. 4) São Paulo's Trade and Futures market (BM&F) is the sixth largest in the world according to "Futures and Option World" Magazine's annual report. It follows only the Chicago stock market, the English Life, the New York stock market, and the French Matisse. It is ahead of the Osaka market (which is seventh in size) and London's market (eighth). In 1994, US$110 billion in stocks were negotiated though financial transactions that mobilizes US$1.58 trillion.

During these years that will follow the ongoing of the Brazilian economy, this financial system will play a key role: that of finding resources both in the country and outside Brazil for giving new wind to investments in Brazil and to the growth of the Brazilian economy.

Brazil's compliance with foreign debt agreements places it in the international capital circuit, making new, long term loans more readily available. Furthermore, the doing away of prejudice so as to allow for the participation of foreign capital in the Brazilian economy through changes provided for in the new constitution, creates an attractive environment for large volumes of foreign investments.

The financial market also contains the process of privatization of state-owned companies. The process of privatization of the metallurgical sector was an enormous success and this process is expected to be revitalized in the second semester of 1995 when the sale of chemical, petrochemical and electrical companies are to be concluded.

It is becoming very clear to investors that the Brazilian environment is a very favorable one. In 1995, the price of stocks were still relatively low, and the potential for development added to the political stability of the country are reassuring. A most varied set of options is available in the stock market, from gigantic corporations, such as Vale do Rio Doce (mining) to solid mid-sized companies

Eletronic banking

Itaú Bank

Banco de Crédito Nacional's financial operations bureau

such as Bardela (capital goods), or Sadia (food). However, the main focus of attraction continues to be, without a doubt, the electric and telecommunication sectors. The privatization of the energy distributing companies and telecommunication companies has been the result of necessity: the Union and the states can no longer afford to make the necessary investments to satisfy consumer demand. This is why there has been more interest in Telebrás stocks and in the stocks of the state subsidiaries such as Telesp, Telerj and Telemig.

There is a very well publicized thesis stating that in this end of century, telecommunication stock is,

globally, among the more profitable investments. In the specific cases of Brazil and São Paulo, there is a strong potential market, since only 10% of the population makes use of this type of service (as opposed to 20% in Portugal, 43% in Japan and 53% in the United States). Furthermore, the market price of stock in these companies continues in 1995 to be lower than their patrimonial value.

There are strong indicators suggesting that the financial heart of Brazil will skip a beat when these papers reach their true value.

1. Source: Revista: *Exame/ Melhores e Maiores*

Chase Manhatan

World Trade Center

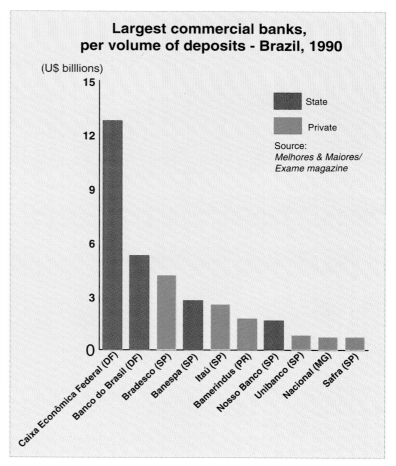

Largest commercial banks,
per volume of deposits - Brazil, 1990

(U$ billlions)

15

12

9

6

3

0

State
Private

Source:
*Melhores & Maiores/
Exame magazine*

Caixa Econômica Federal (DF)
Banco do Brasil (DF)
Bradesco (SP)
Banespa (SP)
Itaú (SP)
Bamerindus (PR)
Nosso Banco (SP)
Unibanco (SP)
Nacional (MG)
Safra (SP)

SÃO PAULO